"Come

two labyrinth walks
using meditations on the
San Damiano Cross

prepared by
Timothy J. Ray

To
Rosalyn A. Knowles Ferrell

a soul-friend and ever-encouraging companion
on many journeys to the center of my spiritual life

Table of Contents

Preface

Prayer often takes us on journeys we do not anticipate, leading us along unexpected paths where we discover hidden joys. Certainly, this was the case as these meditations took form. They began as moments of intense prayer during a 30-day retreat that I wished to share in a weekend of recollection, but they eventually evolved into a more intense spiritual encounter intended to be experienced in a single moment of prayer. At each stage of their development, these meditations distilled the essence of their previous manifestation — offering new spiritual pleasures and insights in each new incarnation.

These meditations began as a challenge offered in prayer when I found myself praying in front of a replica of the San Damiano Cross associated with Saint Francis of Assisi's conversion. During a particularly intense moment in my retreat, I entered a chapel in which I had been praying during the previous days but found that it was already occupied. So, seeking solitude, I entered another chapel and found myself sitting in front of a meter-high reproduction of the San Damiano Cross. In my frustration, I half-jokingly said to the cross before beginning my prayer, "You spoke to Francis, so perhaps you will speak to me." During the next two days, the cross did indeed speak to me as it revealed the essence of my spiritual desires and vocation.

Shortly after my retreat, I created a weekend of recollection based on my encounter with the San Damiano Cross but I remained dissatisfied in sharing my experience until I was asked to create a sequence of guided meditations for a labyrinth walk. The form and intensity of this type of prayer required that I reshape the insights of my prayer. The constraints of time forced me to simplify the language of my presentation so I could express the essential spiritual gifts I received from the cross. But the physical process of the labyrinth — a two-fold journey toward the center and back out again — also made me aware of aspects of my experience I had not yet fully recognized.

So, in gratitude for the many gifts and insights I have received at every stage along my journey with the San Damiano Cross, I pray you also will be blessed with your own spiritual rewards and pleasures while you listen to the wisdom of this special cross.

Acknowledgements

Special thanks to Rev. David Teschner and the members of the Order of the Magi at Christ and Grace Episcopal Church (in Petersburg, Virginia), for whom these meditations were first created.

It also is important for me to acknowledge the gift of the two-volume *St. Francis of Assisi: English Omnibus of the Sources for the Life of St. Francis* that I received from the Franciscan Press, which proved invaluable in developing the opening and closing prayers for the communal liturgy in this project as well as in aiding my broader explorations of the life and prayer of Saint Francis.

Finally, thanks to the Division of Christian Education of the National Council of the Churches of Christ in the United States of America for permission to use biblical citations from the *New Revised Standard Version Bible: with the Apocrypha* (New York: Harper Bibles, 1989) in the preparation of these meditations.

The Cross and the Labyrinth

approaching the San Damiano Cross

The Cross and the Labyrinth

approaching the San Damiano Cross

Like all icons, the San Damiano Cross that Saint Francis encountered in a dilapidated church depicts an eternal moment. The Romanesque artist who created the cross would have seen the painting as an expression of the Incarnation — a mystery of Christian faith in which Jesus is both human and divine as God enters history to free humanity from the burden of sin. For that reason, the cross shows Jesus both crucified and risen with a variety of images surrounding Christ that echo the glory of that transformative moment. As an act of revelation, the painting shows this event from the unchanging perspective of God.

On the other hand, the journey in and out of the labyrinth represents a very human need. Traveling to the center of the labyrinth, we put aside our daily concerns in order to reach out to God in prayer. This inward journey involves becoming aware of the aspects of our lives that have taken us away from God's desires as well as seeking to transcend these limitations so we may hear God's voice more clearly. Arriving at the center, both of the labyrinth and of ourselves, we express our deepest needs and desires in quiet prayer before beginning the outward pilgrimage that returns us to our daily lives as transformed instruments of God's redemptive action in the world.

In bringing these two events together, these meditations offer an opportunity for us to encounter the eternal event shown on the San Damiano Cross through a very human act of prayer shaped by the experience of the labyrinth. During the inward journey, the meditations invite us to reflect on the ways in which the images on the cross express our needs as we approach God. Then, arriving at the center, we are asked to consider the totality of the cross and the ways in which God speaks to us through it. Finally, on the outward journey, the meditations challenge us to consider the ways in which the images we already encountered express God's desire for us to change the world in which we live.

These meditations are not theological reflections on the cross and its symbolism. Instead, they are a journey of prayer in which we are invited to express our own neediness and to experience God's sustaining presence in our lives. So, like Saint Francis before us, we should approach the cross with humility and confidence as God speaks to us through its images — asking us to become transformative signs of God's loving activity in our own lives and in the lives of the people (and other creatures of God) we daily encounter. Approached with this simplicity of heart, our encounter with the San Damiano Cross on the labyrinth may transform us as it has so many others.

"Come to Me"

---

a prayer service and labyrinth walk
using the San Damiano Cross
and the prayers of Francis of Assisi

Preparation

Before presenting the prayer service for your community, you should take some time to consider the following issues:

• The Guides for the Service

In addition to the leader of this prayer service, you will need two people to read the meditations. Also, if you choose to incorporate music into the service, you will need to gather the musicians and make arrangements to bring their instruments to the labyrinth or arrange for presenting the music electronically. Finally, if you choose not to provide the congregation with images from the San Damiano Cross, you will need another person to project the images from the cross during the labyrinth walk.

• The Location of the Labyrinth

Almost all of your choices in the presentation of the prayer service will be shaped by the location of the labyrinth you are using. You will have greater flexibility in your choices if it is indoors. Access to electricity will allow you to use projections during the service and an enclosed space will allow you to present readings and music without external distractions. However, if the labyrinth is located outdoors, you will need to decide what resources are available to help you create a contemplative space for the prayer service.

• The Length of the Service

Since its opening and closing prayers are quite brief, the prayer service's length will be determined by the amount of time you decide to allow for the members of your community to walk on the labyrinth. Once you have made this decision, the meditations on the San Damiano Cross should be evenly spaced within the time you allocate so you are able to preserve a distinct boundary between each meditation as well as to create a balance between speaking and silence during this part of the service.

• The Placement of the Participants

If possible, the musical and prayer leaders should be placed on the side opposite the labyrinth's entrance and the community should be positioned in front of its entrance. Chairs should be provided for the participants and spaced far enough apart that individuals may easily leave their seats to walk on the labyrinth. Also, everyone involved in the prayer service should be close enough to the labyrinth to hear the words and music of the service — especially the meditations during the labyrinth walk.

• The Images from the San Damiano Cross

It is important to determine how to present the images from the San Damiano Cross without distracting the participants during the service. You should choose whether to present the images using a digital projector or through printed hand-outs. These images are an essential aspect of the service, so you should be careful to make certain that everyone has easy access to them — whether on the labyrinth or in their seats.

Note: *If you use a digital projector, you should be careful to maintain a clear line of sight for the images for all participants as well as to avoid casting shadows across the images. This may require additional preparation time as you decide where and how to best project the images.*

• Programs for the Prayer Service

You will find folders containing print-ready programs and other digital resources for the prayer services at:

http://resources.silentheron.net.

These digital resources are prepared in zip files containing folders indicating the paper size you will need to use to prepare the program for the prayer service (i.e., US letterhead and A4).

Each program folder contains instructions for printing and preparing the two options for the program. These folders also include the meditations on the cross for the readers and images from the San Damiano Cross designed to be distributed as hand-outs at the service (if digital projections are not used). All of these materials are prepared in PDF format.

Additional folders on the resource site include high resolution images from the San Damiano Cross for digital projection (prepared both individually and as a PowerPoint presentation) as well as materials for the virtual labyrinth walk option presented later in this book prepared in PDF format.

• The Music for the Service

While particular types of songs are suggested for each part of the prayer service, it is especially important to select a hymn at the end of the labyrinth walk that echoes the call to service in the final meditation (such as "The Peace Prayer of Saint Francis"). Since the San Damiano Cross is associated with Saint Francis, you also may want to select hymns that reflect his spiritual vision (i.e., love of nature, devotion to peace, etc.).

Also, you will need to decide how comfortable the participants in the prayer service will be during the silent periods of the labyrinth walk. If necessary (and possible), you may choose to play instrumental music during or between the meditations.

• Individuals not Walking the Labyrinth

Finally, you should decide how you want to engage individuals unable (or unwilling) to enter the labyrinth during the prayer service's labyrinth walk.

This may involve inviting them to engage the meditations prayerfully during the labyrinth walk or offering them blank labyrinths (available on the resource site in the folder for the virtual labyrinth walk) to use in their seats.

You also may want to create a special section of seats for individuals who do not (or cannot) participate in the labyrinth walk.

"Come to Me"
_____

a prayer service and labyrinth walk

When the community is gathered around the labyrinth, a bell (or other signal) should indicate the beginning of the service. If possible, all members of the community should stand.

An Opening Hymn (optional)

Opening Prayer

Leader:
You are holy, Lord, the only God,

All:
And Your deeds are wonderful.

Leader:
You are strong.
You are great.
You are the Most High.

All:
You are Almighty.

Leader:
You, Holy Father are King of heaven and earth.

You are Three and One, Lord God, all Good.
You are Good, all Good, supreme Good.

All:
Lord God, living and true.

Leader:
You are love. You are wisdom.
You are humility. You are endurance.
You are rest. You are peace.

All:
You are joy and gladness.

Leader:
You are justice and moderation.
You are all our riches, and You suffice for us.
You are beauty.

All:
You are gentleness.

Leader:
You are our protector.
You are our guardian and defender.
You are our courage. You are our haven and our hope.

All:
You are our faith, our great consolation.

Leader:

You are our eternal life, Great and Wonderful Lord.

All:

God Almighty, Merciful Savior.

A Hymn of Thanksgiving (optional)

The members of the community should be invited to sit.

Labyrinth Walk

Leader:

In 1205, a young Francesco Bernardone came to pray at the small and dilapidated San Damiano Church outside the town of Assisi in central Italy. Traumatized by his experiences of war and disowned by his family, he was in the midst of a profound spiritual crisis as he knelt before the iconic cross in the sanctuary.

During one period of intense prayer, he heard the Christ on the cross say, "Francesco, go repair my church which is falling into ruins." Responding to that voice, Francesco Bernardone found inner peace and discovered his life-purpose — going on to become one of the most beloved Christian saints, Francis of Assisi.

You are now invited to enter and walk this labyrinth, or to remain in your seats, listening to what this cross may say to you.

Occasionally during the labyrinth walk, the community will be asked to stop walking and to stand still while meditations based on the San Damiano Cross are presented.

1. Acknowledge God's blessings in your life.

Reader 1:
Pause for a moment and be still. (Pause) Acknowledge God's blessings in your life. (Pause) As you begin, take a moment to look at the image at the top of the cross. See the hand of God descending from heaven, giving His blessing … and see the company of saints singing God's praises.

Hear the words of 1 Peter 2: 1-5 —

"Rid yourselves, therefore, of all malice, and all guile, insincerity, envy, and all slander. Like newborn infants, long for the pure, spiritual milk, so that by it you may grow into salvation — if indeed you have tasted that the Lord is good.

"Come to him, a living stone, though rejected by mortals yet chosen and precious in God's sight, and like

14

living stones, let yourselves be built into a spiritual house, to be a holy priesthood, to offer spiritual sacrifices acceptable to God through Jesus Christ."

As you continue your journey, consider these things and ask … Where is God's blessing in your life? Think of the times when you have felt God's hand upon you, supporting and sanctifying you. What debt of gratitude do you feel for God's generosity?

2. Accept Christ's embrace.

Reader 2:
Pause again and be still. (Pause) Accept Christ's embrace. (Pause) See the image of Christ on the cross, with his arms spread wide.

He is welcoming you and asking that you allow him to embrace you. Allow yourself to trust Christ and to accept his embrace as you listen to his invitation in Matthew 11: 28-30 —

"Come to me, all you that are weary and are carrying heavy burdens, and I will give you rest. Take my yoke upon you, and learn from me; for I am gentle and humble in heart, and you will find rest for your souls. For my yoke is easy, and my burden is light."

As you continue your journey, consider these things and ask … Where do you need the embrace of Christ? Where do you feel weakest and most in need of his support?

3. Be transformed by the companionship of Christ.

Reader 1:
Pause again and be still. (Pause) Be transformed by the companionship of Christ. (Pause) Contemplate the figures under Christ's arms. The image appears to be out of balance.

Why are there only two people on one side and three on the other? Because Christ is making room for you. In Christ's heart, there is always room for one more person in need as he offers each of us a new life as his companion.

Hear Saint Paul's admonition in Romans 12: 1-2 —

"I appeal to you therefore, brothers and sisters, by the mercies of God, to present your bodies as a living sacrifice, holy and acceptable to God, which is your spiritual worship. Do not be conformed to this world, but be transformed by the renewing of your minds, so that you may discern what is the will of God — what is good and acceptable and perfect."

As you continue your journey, consider these things and ask … Where are you most alone and vulnerable? What does Christ's companionship mean to you? How does this change your life? How does it make you feel to know that Christ loves you?

4. See the wounds that Christ suffered for you.

Reader 2:
Pause again and be still. (Pause) See the wounds that Christ suffered for you. (Pause) Look at the wounds on Christ's hands and feet. These are the wounds that he bore for you.

Take a moment to feel sorrow for Christ's sacrifice for you … and to feel gratitude for Christ's generosity.

In a spirit of penance, reflect on 1 Peter 2: 23-25 —

"When he was abused, he did not return abuse; when he suffered, he did not threaten; but he entrusted himself to the one who judges justly. He himself bore our sins in his body on the cross, so that, free from sins, we might live for righteousness; by his wounds you have been healed. For you were going astray like sheep, but now you have returned to the shepherd and guardian of your souls."

As you continue your journey, consider these things and ask … How have you wounded Christ? How do you continue to harm him? How can you make amends?

5. Rejoice in Christ's Resurrection!

Reader 1:
Pause again and be still. (Pause) Rejoice in Christ's Resurrection! (Pause) Stop for a moment to reflect on the image as a whole. See now that it is an image of the Resurrection. Christ stands in front of the Cross — risen and alive! Say a prayer of humility as you acknowledge the love Christ shows in redeeming you.

Take a moment to recall your feelings and prayers on your inward journey. Say a prayer of dedication as you promise to respond to Christ in others as Christ did for you.

Then, listen to the words of Colossians 3: 12-14 —

"As God's chosen ones, holy and beloved, clothe yourselves with compassion, kindness, humility, meekness, and patience. Bear with one another and, if anyone has a complaint against another, forgive each other; just as the Lord has forgiven you, so you also must forgive. Above all, clothe yourselves with love, which binds everything together in perfect harmony."

As you continue your journey, consider these things and ask … What does Christ's Resurrection mean to you? Where do you need resurrection? Where can you be a sign of resurrection to others?

6. Seek out the wounded.

Reader 2:

Pause again and be still. (Pause) Seek out the wounded. (Pause) Look again at the wounds of Christ. They continue to bleed … in the poor, the suffering, and the needy … in the destruction of God's creation, the abuse and pollution of natural environments, and the extinctions of animal and plant species.

Contemplate the words of Philippians 2: 1-5 —

"If then there is any encouragement in Christ, any consolation from love, any sharing in the Spirit, any compassion and sympathy, make my joy complete: be of the same mind, having the same love, being in full accord and of one mind. Do nothing from selfish ambition or conceit, but in humility regard others as better than yourselves. Let each of you look not to your own interests, but to the interests of others. Let the same mind be in you that was in Christ Jesus."

As you continue your journey, consider these things and ask … Where does Christ continue to bleed in the world around you? In the lives of other men and women? In the abuse of God's creation? Where can you be the hands and feet of Christ in our world?

Ask God to help you to seek out the wounded in your world, both human and nonhuman, so they may experience the love and generosity of Christ through you.

7. Befriend the lonely.

Reader 1:
Pause again and be still. (Pause) Befriend the lonely. (Pause) Look again at the images under the arms of Christ. Christ offers his friendship and love to the lonely and the needy.

Hear Christ's parable in Matthew 25: 34-40, when Jesus said —

"Then the king will say, 'Come, you that are blessed by my Father, inherit the kingdom prepared for you from the foundation of the world; for I was hungry and you gave me food, I was thirsty and you gave me something to drink, I was a stranger and you welcomed me, I was naked and you gave me clothing, I was sick and you took care of me, I was in prison and you visited me.' Then the righteous will answer him, 'Lord, when was it that we saw you hungry and gave you food, or thirsty

and gave you something to drink? And when was it that we saw you a stranger and welcomed you, or naked and gave you clothing? And when was it that we saw you sick or in prison and visited you?' And the king will answer them, 'Truly I tell you, just as you did it to one of the least of these who are members of my family, you did it to me.'

As you continue your journey, consider these things and ask … Where can you offer friendship to others? To whom could you be a sign of Christ's offer of true friendship?

Ask God to help you reach out to the lonely so they may feel the companionship of Christ.

8. Embrace the suffering.

Reader 2:
Pause again and be still. (Pause) Embrace the suffering. (Pause) Look again at the image of Christ, with his arms outstretched in embrace. You are Christ to others when you act on his behalf.

Reflect on the assertion in James 2: 14-17 —

"What good is it, my brothers and sisters, if you say you have faith but do not have works? Can faith save you? If a brother or sister is naked and lacks daily food, and

one of you says to them, "Go in peace; keep warm and eat your fill," and yet you do not supply their bodily needs, what is the good of that? So faith by itself, if it has no works, is dead."

As you continue your journey, consider these things and ask … Who or what do you know that needs the embrace of Christ, offering his consolation and comfort? Who or what do you know who is suffering … a man or woman in pain, mental or physical … a part of God's nonhuman creation, distressed or dying?

Ask God to help you embrace the suffering in and of the world, becoming a sign of Christ's love to the world.

9. Live for the glory of God.

Leader:
Please leave the labyrinth. Look again at the image at the top of the cross. See God's hand blessing you … and the saints inviting you to praise God with them through your own acts of service and love. May we all live for the glory of God.

There is a brief period of silence as members of the community return to their seats.

A Hymn of Dedication (optional)

Closing Prayer and Blessing

The members of the community should be invited to stand.

Leader:
Let us take a moment to say this prayer written in the spirit of Francis:

All:
Lord, make me an instrument of your peace,
Where there is hatred, let me sow love;
where there is injury, pardon;
where there is doubt, faith;
where there is despair, hope;
where there is darkness, light;
where there is sadness, joy;
O Divine Master, grant that I may not so much seek to
be consoled as to console;
to be understood as to understand;
to be loved as to love.
For it is in giving that we receive;
it is in pardoning that we are pardoned;
and it is in dying that we are born to eternal life.

Leader:
As we return to our daily lives, know that we are not alone. Christ will continue to walk with us — as he does with countless other Christians — as we reach out to

others and bring Christ's healing presence to a world in need.

May you become signs of Christ's continuing presence in the world, remembering the words of 1 Thessalonians 5: 16-18 — "Rejoice always, pray without ceasing, give thanks in all circumstances; for this is the will of God in Christ Jesus for you."

All:
For this is the will of God in Christ Jesus for us.

Leader:
Most high, glorious God, enlighten the darkness of our hearts and give us, Lord, a correct faith, a certain hope, a perfect charity, sense and knowledge, so that we may carry out Your holy and true command.

All:
Amen.

A Concluding Hymn (optional)

The members of the community are welcome to continue their reflections, either in their seats or by returning to the labyrinth, before dispersing in silence.

.

"Come to Me"

a private labyrinth walk
using the San Damiano Cross

Preparation

These meditations offer a contemplative labyrinth walk based on the images of the San Damiano Cross. Still, there are two tasks you will need to complete before you begin:

• Placing Markers along the Way

If the labyrinth you are using is not already marked, you will need to select five small objects (e.g., index cards, stones, tiles, etc.) and place these markers at even intervals along the path of the labyrinth. Begin by placing the first marker at the entrance of the labyrinth. Next, walk to the center of the labyrinth while counting your steps and place another marker in the center. Then, walking out of the labyrinth in the same manner you entered, position the remaining markers one-quarter, one-half and three-quarters of your way out of the labyrinth as you walk.

• Selecting Music for the Walk (if desired)

You may want to create a playlist for your journey in and out of the labyrinth if you think you might be disturbed by the sounds around you or you feel uncomfortable with extended periods of silence. If so, choose a selection of quiet instrumental music that will not distract you as you pray. You may also decide to include recordings using ambient sounds of nature so that you feel God's presence in creation during your walk on the labyrinth.

If you decide to use music during your labyrinth walk, allow yourself to slowly enter into the world of the music before you begin the first meditation. You also should listen to the music for a short time after you finish the final meditation as you leave the labyrinth. In this way, the music becomes another marker in the sacred space of your labyrinth walk.

Considerations

In 1205, a young Francesco Bernardone came to pray at the small and dilapidated San Damiano Church outside the town of Assisi in central Italy. Traumatized by his experiences of war and disowned by his family, he was in the midst of a profound spiritual crisis as he knelt before the iconic cross in the sanctuary. During one period of intense prayer, he heard the Christ on the cross say, "Francesco, go repair my church which is falling into ruins." Responding to that voice, Francesco Bernardone found inner peace and discovered his life-purpose — going on to become one of the most beloved Christian saints, Francis of Assisi.

These meditations invite you to listen to what this cross may say to you. They are not intended to explain the detailed iconography of the San Damiano Cross. Instead, they are meant to serve as a guide to imaginative prayer — allowing particular aspects of the cross to speak in their unique way to each person using them.

So, before you begin, consider the following suggestions:

• Allow the labyrinth to guide you. The path will take you to the labyrinth's center and back again, so you cannot get lost.

• Walk slowly at a comfortable and even pace. This will help you become more meditative and reflective.

• Free yourself from your daily concerns. By focusing on each step you make in the labyrinth, you will allow God's Spirit to direct your thoughts and prayers.

• Trust that you are not walking alone. Your journey into the labyrinth is an act of prayer. God will be with you — listening to your needs and guiding your steps.

• Approach the cross intuitively. Allow your mind to wander and linger on the parts of the cross that speak most strongly to you.

• Do not worry about the "meaning" of the cross. Francis would not have known all the images on the cross when he prayed in front of it. So, why should you?

• Be guided by the cross on your own unique spiritual journey. God's Spirit will help you find your own meaning in the images from the cross. Trust and follow those impulses.

With these thoughts in mind, you are almost ready to begin your journey. So, before entering the labyrinth, imagine yourself doing the following:

• Standing at the entrance to the labyrinth at the first marker. Quiet your spirit and, when you are prepared, read the first meditation. Then, take a moment to reflect on the meditation before walking slowly and prayerfully into the labyrinth toward the second marker.

• On arriving at the second marker, stop to slowly read and reflect on the second meditation before continuing along the labyrinth's path to the next marker.

• Follow this pattern until you reach the center of the labyrinth. After reading and reflecting on the fifth meditation, take an additional moment to recall your experiences at the earlier markers and the prayers associated with each.

• Following the same pattern as before, stop at each marker to pray the corresponding meditations until you reach the exit of the labyrinth. At the final marker, read and reflect on the final meditation.

• When you are finished with your reflection, turn around and look at the labyrinth. Then, consider your overall prayer experience before leaving.

Now, when you are ready, begin your labyrinth walk using the meditations provided in the following pages.

"Come to Me"

---

a private labyrinth walk

During your walk, you will come to a series of numbered stations. Each of these corresponds to a meditation in this booklet containing a detailed image from the San Damiano Cross, a short reflection on that image and a scriptural verse.

At each station, take a moment to read the meditation and consider the image from the cross. Then, continue your walk through the labyrinth — allowing the parts of the meditation and image to emerge that speak most strongly to you.

Be certain to stop your contemplation of each meditation when you reach the next station. If you find yourself unable to do this, then put aside these meditations and allow God's Spirit to guide you on your journey through the labyrinth.

1. Acknowledge God's blessings in your life.

As you begin, take a moment to look at the image at the top of the cross.

See the hand of God descending from heaven, giving His blessing … and see the company of saints singing God's praises. Praise God, saying:

You are holy, Lord, the only God,
And Your deeds are wonderful.
You, Holy Father are King of heaven and earth.
You are Three and One, Lord God, all Good.
Lord God, living and true.

You are love. You are wisdom.
You are humility. You are endurance.
You are rest. You are peace.
You are joy and gladness.

You are justice and moderation.

You are our protector.
You are our guardian and defender.
You are our courage. You are our haven and our hope.
You are our faith, our great consolation.
You are our eternal life, Great and Wonderful Lord,
God Almighty, Merciful Savior.
Amen.

Then, consider the words of 1 Peter 2: 1-5 —

"Rid yourselves, therefore, of all malice, and all guile, insincerity, envy, and all slander. Like newborn infants, long for the pure, spiritual milk, so that by it you may grow into salvation — if indeed you have tasted that the Lord is good.

"Come to him, a living stone, though rejected by mortals yet chosen and precious in God's sight, and like living stones, let yourselves be built into a spiritual house, to be a holy priesthood, to offer spiritual sacrifices acceptable to God through Jesus Christ."

Where is God's blessing in your life? Think of the times when you have felt God's hand upon you, supporting and sanctifying you. What debt of gratitude do you feel for God's generosity?

2. Accept Christ's embrace.

Consider the image of Christ on the cross, with his arms spread wide.

He is welcoming you and asking that you allow him to embrace you. Allow yourself to trust Christ and to accept his embrace as you hear his invitation in Matthew 11: 28-30 —

"Come to me, all you that are weary and are carrying heavy burdens, and I will give you rest. Take my yoke upon you, and learn from me; for I am gentle and humble in heart, and you will find rest for your souls. For my yoke is easy, and my burden is light."

Where do you need the embrace of Christ? Where do you feel weakest and most in need of his support?

3. Be transformed by the companionship of Christ.

Contemplate the figures under Christ's arms. The image appears to be out of balance.

Why are there only two people on one side and three on the other? Because Christ is making room for you. In Christ's heart, there is always room for one more person in need as he offers each of us a new life as his companion.

Consider Saint Paul's admonition in Romans 12: 1-2 —

"I appeal to you therefore, brothers and sisters, by the mercies of God, to present your bodies as a living sacrifice, holy and acceptable to God, which is your spiritual worship. Do not be conformed to this world, but be transformed by the renewing of your minds, so

35

that you may discern what is the will of God — what is good and acceptable and perfect."

Where are you most alone and vulnerable? What does Christ's companionship mean to you? How does this change your life? How does it make you feel to know that Christ loves you?

4. See the wounds that Christ suffered for you.

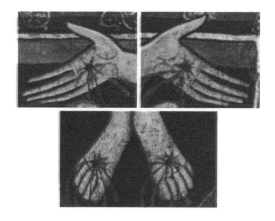

Look at the wounds on Christ's hands and feet. These are the wounds that he bore for you.

Take a moment to feel sorrow for Christ's sacrifice for you … and to feel gratitude for Christ's generosity.

In a spirit of penance, reflect on 1 Peter 2: 23-25 —

"When he was abused, he did not return abuse; when he suffered, he did not threaten; but he entrusted himself to the one who judges justly. He himself bore our sins in his body on the cross, so that, free from sins, we might live for righteousness; by his wounds you have been healed. For you were going astray like sheep, but now you have returned to the shepherd and guardian of your souls."

How have you wounded Christ? How do you continue to harm him? How can you make amends?

5. Rejoice in Christ's Resurrection!

As you reach the center of the labyrinth, stop for a moment to reflect on the image as a whole. See now that it is an image of the Resurrection. Christ stands in front of the Cross — risen and alive! Say a prayer of humility as you acknowledge the love Christ shows in redeeming you.

Take a moment to recall your feelings and prayers on your inward journey.

Then, walk around the labyrinth's inner circle, saying a prayer of gratitude for Christ's self-sacrificing love for you.

As you leave the center of the labyrinth, say a prayer of dedication as you promise to respond to Christ in others as Christ did for you.

Reflect on the words of Colossians 3: 12-14 —

"As God's chosen ones, holy and beloved, clothe yourselves with compassion, kindness, humility, meekness, and patience. Bear with one another and, if anyone has a complaint against another, forgive each other; just as the Lord has forgiven you, so you also must forgive. Above all, clothe yourselves with love, which binds everything together in perfect harmony."

What does Christ's Resurrection mean to you? Where do you need resurrection? Where can you be a sign of resurrection to others?

6. Seek out the wounded.

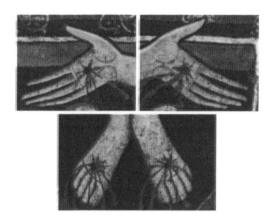

Look again at the wounds of Christ. They continue to bleed … in the poor, the suffering, and the needy … in the destruction of God's creation, the abuse and pollution of natural environments, and the extinctions of animal and plant species.

Contemplate the words of Philippians 2: 1-5 —

"If then there is any encouragement in Christ, any consolation from love, any sharing in the Spirit, any compassion and sympathy, make my joy complete: be of the same mind, having the same love, being in full accord and of one mind. Do nothing from selfish ambition or conceit, but in humility regard others as better than yourselves. Let each of you look not to your own interests, but to the interests of others. Let the same mind be in you that was in Christ Jesus."

Where does Christ continue to bleed in the world around you? In the lives of other men and women? In the abuse of God's creation? Where can you be the hands and feet of Christ in our world?

Ask God to help you to seek out the wounded in your world, both human and nonhuman, so they may experience the love and generosity of Christ through you.

7. Befriend the lonely.

Look again at the images under the arms of Christ. Christ offers his friendship and love to the lonely and the needy.

Consider Christ's parable in Matthew 25: 34-40 when Jesus said —

"Then the king will say, 'Come, you that are blessed by my Father, inherit the kingdom prepared for you from the foundation of the world; for I was hungry and you gave me food, I was thirsty and you gave me something to drink, I was a stranger and you welcomed me, I was naked and you gave me clothing, I was sick and you took care of me, I was in prison and you visited me.' Then the righteous will answer him, 'Lord, when was it that we saw you hungry and gave you food, or thirsty and gave you something to drink? And when was it that

we saw you a stranger and welcomed you, or naked and gave you clothing? And when was it that we saw you sick or in prison and visited you?' And the king will answer them, 'Truly I tell you, just as you did it to one of the least of these who are members of my family, you did it to me.'

Where can you offer friendship to others? To whom could you be a sign of Christ's offer of true friendship?

Ask God to help you reach out to the lonely so they may feel the companionship of Christ.

8. Embrace the suffering.

Look again at the image of Christ, with his arms outstretched in embrace. You are Christ to others when you act on his behalf.

Reflect on the assertion in James 2: 14-17 —

"What good is it, my brothers and sisters, if you say you have faith but do not have works? Can faith save you? If a brother or sister is naked and lacks daily food, and one of you says to them, "Go in peace; keep warm and eat your fill," and yet you do not supply their bodily needs, what is the good of that? So faith by itself, if it has no works, is dead."

Who or what do you know that needs the embrace of Christ, offering his consolation and comfort? Who or what do you know who is suffering … a man or woman in pain, mental or physical … a part of God's nonhuman creation, distressed or dying?

Ask God to help you embrace the suffering in and of the world, becoming a sign of Christ's love to the world.

9. Live for the glory of God.

As you leave the labyrinth, look again at the image at the top of the cross. See God's hand blessing you … and the saints inviting you to praise God with them through acts of service and love.

Then, take a moment to say this prayer written in the spirit of Francis:

Lord, make me an instrument of your peace,
Where there is hatred, let me sow love;
where there is injury, pardon;
where there is doubt, faith;
where there is despair, hope;
where there is darkness, light;
where there is sadness, joy;
O Divine Master, grant that I may not so much seek to
be consoled as to console;

to be understood as to understand;
to be loved as to love.
For it is in giving that we receive;
it is in pardoning that we are pardoned;
and it is in dying that we are born to eternal life.
Amen.

As you return to your daily life, know that you are not alone. Christ will continue to walk with you – as he does with countless other Christians — as you reach out to others and bring Christ's healing presence to a world in need.

Be a sign of Christ's continuing presence in the world, remembering the words of 1 Thessalonians 5: 16-18 …

"Rejoice always, pray without ceasing, give thanks in all circumstances; for this is the will of God in Christ Jesus for you."

A Virtual Labyrinth Walk

Preparation

If you are unable to walk (or visit) a physical labyrinth, you will be able to conduct a private labyrinth walk – alone or with others – using the illustrations provided in the following pages.

These images (as well as unmarked versions of the same labyrinths) are available online at:
http://resources.silentheron.net
Prepared in PDF format, these files are in zip files containing folders indicating the paper size (i.e., US letterhead or A4) needed to print the images correctly.

Note: *The unmarked versions of the various labyrinth types also make it possible for everyone to participate in the prayer service presented earlier in this book. However, in order to maintain this common journey, it is important that the version of the labyrinth mirror the one being used by the rest of the community.*

If you choose to use these images, your preparation should involve:

• Deciding which version of the labyrinth to use
If you are using the images on your own, you may choose the labyrinth you like best. However, if you are using the illustrations with others, it is important that you have a common experience of entering and leaving the labyrinth, especially if you use music or shared prayers during your virtual labyrinth walk.

• Determining how you will trace your progress

It is very important that you physically trace your journey in and out of the labyrinth, either with your finger or with a small pointer (e.g., a toothpick, a paper clip, etc.). On a practical level, this will help you avoid losing your way on the small path presented in the image. However, on an emotional and spiritual level, tracing your progress in the labyrinth will reinforce the connection between your prayer and the physical action in entering and leaving the labyrinth.

Also, while tracing your journey in the labyrinth, be careful not to travel too quickly. If you were walking the labyrinth, you would proceed slowly and deliberately (i.e., step by step). So, it is important to find a way to bring this conscious "slowing down" to your virtual experience – either through your breathing or re-reading an aspect of the meditation (e.g., the scripture reading, part of the subsequent prayer), etc.) word-by-word (with a slight pause between each) as you move toward the next meditation.

• Reviewing the considerations for a labyrinth walk

Using the images allows you to have the same experience as anyone who is walking the labyrinth, so it is important that you review the considerations presented earlier in this book for the private labyrinth walk and follow the instructions concerning the process of engaging the meditations while in the labyrinth before using the meditations from the private labyrinth for your own journey.

In this illustration, the markers correspond to the following meditations:

(A)   Meditations 1 and 9.
(B)   Meditations 2 and 8.
(C)   Meditations 3 and 7.
(D)   Meditations 4 and 6.
(E)   Meditation 5.

In this illustration, the markers correspond to the following meditations:

(A)   Meditations 1 and 9.
(B)   Meditations 2 and 8.
(C)   Meditations 3 and 7.
(D)   Meditations 4 and 6.
(E)   Meditation 5.

In this illustration, the markers correspond to the following meditations:

    (A)   Meditations 1 and 9.

    (B)   Meditations 2 and 8.

    (C)   Meditations 3 and 7.

    (D)   Meditations 4 and 6.

    (E)   Meditation 5.

Nurturing the Gifts of the Cross

Nurturing the Gifts of the Cross

In his prayers before the San Damiano Cross, Francis of Assisi came to a profound knowledge of himself and of his vocation in the world. Born into a rich family but traumatized by his experiences of war, Francis embraced a life of poverty made rich by acts of compassion and reconciliation following the example of Jesus. He saw in the world the continuing suffering of Christ, yet he understood — and sought to aid — the redemption of creation made possible through the Resurrection. In the small San Damiano church, Francis' humility allowed him to accept the healing love of God and his gratitude led him to share that love with his fellow creatures, both human and nonhuman.

This transformation did not occur immediately so, as you leave your own encounter with the San Damiano Cross, it also may take time for the graces of your experience to become evident. Just as Francis often returned to the cross in prayer (and carried the memory of those prayers on his many travels), you may find it helpful to record the most significant aspects of your prayer with the San Damiano Cross — either some aspect of the images on the cross or words from the scriptural meditations — and return to these moments in future prayers. These seminal experiences from your time with the San Damiano Cross are seeds of grace to be nurtured and brought to fruition through your devotion and God's abundant love.

Approached with the same humility and gratitude demonstrated by Francis, your continuing attention to these prayers will allow the presence of Christ to touch you in the deepest aspects of your being. Your experiences of pain, confusion through sinful choices or any other form of neediness will be sanctified through the wounds of Jesus and you will acquire through God's grace healing, forgiveness and redemption. So, in these future prayers, it is important to remember that the crucified Christ willingly shares in your woundedness — lifting and carrying your wounds and pain so you may be healed and redeemed.

Still, it is important to remember you are not healed simply for yourself. In your labyrinthine journey with the San Damiano Cross, you were reminded that you are both a unique expression of God's love and a part of a broader realm of redeemed creation being called back to a state of grace. So, the recognition of God's healing and redemptive grace in your own life becomes an invitation to become an instrument of that love by aiding God's other creatures (whether, following the example of Francis, they be human or nonhuman). Healed, but still retaining the marks of your woundedness, you will become a source of hope for others as well as an instrument of God's redemptive activity through your own acts of service and love.

About the Author

Timothy J. Ray brings a diverse background in biblical theology, creative expression, cultural studies and the history of ideas to his work in spiritual direction and formation. He received his Bachelor of Arts, *magna cum laude*, in a multi-disciplinary program focused on the cultural history of law and politics from Niagara University before earning, with distinction, both his Master of Fine Arts in Dramaturgy and Dramatic Criticism from Yale University and his Master of Letters in Theology from the University of Saint Andrews.

In addition to preparing *Come to Me*, he has published *The Carmichael Prayerbook, A Journey to the Land of the Saints*, *A Pilgrimage to the Land of the Saints* and *Seeking our Place of Resurrection*.

For more information about Timothy and his activities, please visit http://www.silentheron.net.

Printed in Great Britain
by Amazon

28468182R00041